D0100112

DENMARK

...in Pictures

Courtesy of Ray Christensen

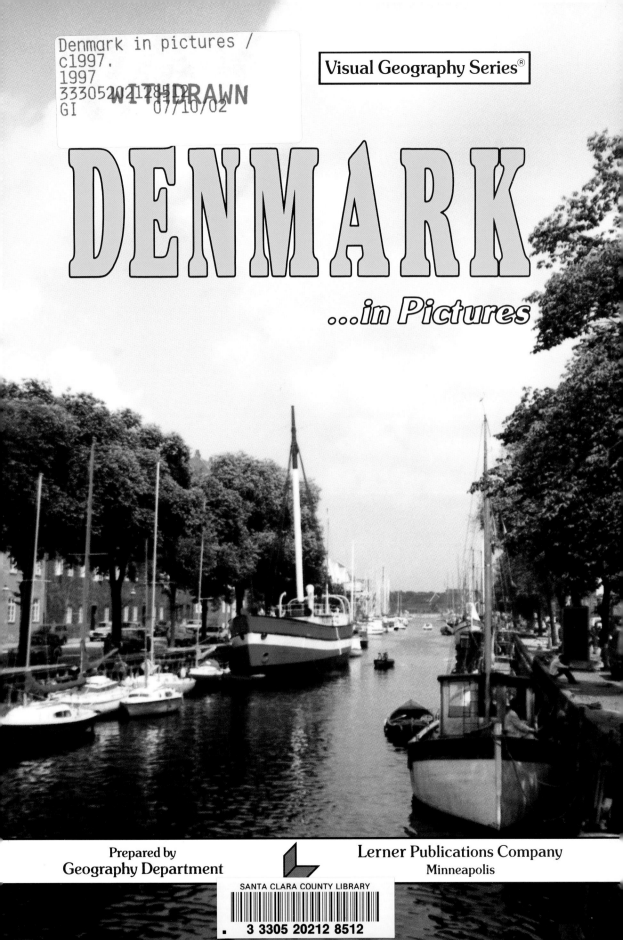

Denmark in pictures /
c1997.
1997
33305202178812
GI   07/10/02

WITHDRAWN

Visual Geography Series®

DENMARK

...in Pictures

Prepared by
Geography Department

Lerner Publications Company
Minneapolis

SANTA CLARA COUNTY LIBRARY

3 3305 20212 8512

Copyright © 1991, 1997 by Lerner Publications Company.

All rights reserved. International copyright secured. No part of this book may be reproduced, stored in a retrieval system, or transmitted in any form or by any means — electronic, mechanical, photocopying, recording, or otherwise — without the prior written permission of the publisher, except for the inclusion of brief quotations in an acknowledged review.

Independent Picture Service

A boat moves between volcanic cliffs on the Faeroe Islands, a distant part of Denmark's territory.

This book is an all-new edition in the Visual Geography Series. Previous editions were published by Sterling Publishing Company, New York City. The text, set in 10/12 Century Textbook, is fully revised and updated, and new photographs, maps, charts, and captions have been added.

LIBRARY OF CONGRESS CATALOGING-IN-PUBLICATION DATA

Denmark in pictures / prepared by Geography Department, Lerner Publications Company.
    p. cm. – (Visual geography series)
    Rev. ed. of: Denmark in pictures / prepared by Toby A. Reiss.
    Includes index.
    Summary: Examines the topography, history, society, economy, and governmental structure of Denmark.
    ISBN 0-8225-1880-5 (lib. bdg.)
    1. Denmark. [1. Denmark.] I. Lerner Publications Company, Geography Dept. II. Series: Visual geography series (Minneapolis, Minn.)
DL109.D435   1991
948.9'0022'2 – dc20   90–41730

International Standard Book Number: 0-8225-1880-5
Library of Congress Catalog Card Number: 90-41730

VISUAL GEOGRAPHY SERIES®

Publisher
Harry Jonas Lerner
Associate Publisher
Nancy M. Campbell
Senior Editor
Mary M. Rodgers
Editors
Gretchen Bratvold
Dan Filbin
Photo Researcher
Kerstin Coyle
Editorial/Photo Assistant
Marybeth Campbell
Consultants/Contributors
John G. Rice
Phyllis Schuster
Sandra K. Davis
Designer
Jim Simondet
Cartographer
Carol F. Barrett
Indexers
Kristine S. Schubert
Sylvia Timian
Production Manager
Gary J. Hansen

Independent Picture Service

A horse-drawn cart follows a waterlogged track along Denmark's coast.

Acknowledgments

Title page photo courtesy of Jill Anderson.

Elevation contours adapted from *The Times Atlas of the World*, seventh comprehensive edition (New York: Times Books, 1985).

Some vowels with accent marks are used in this book. The letter "å" often is pronounced like the combination "aw" in English. "Ø" sounds roughly like the "u" in the English word *hurt*.

3 4 5 6 7 8 9 10 – JR – 04 03 02 01 00 99 98 97

The spire of the Church of Our Savior in Copenhagen has a curving staircase that people can climb to get a spectacular view of the capital city.

Courtesy of Harlan V. Anderson

Contents

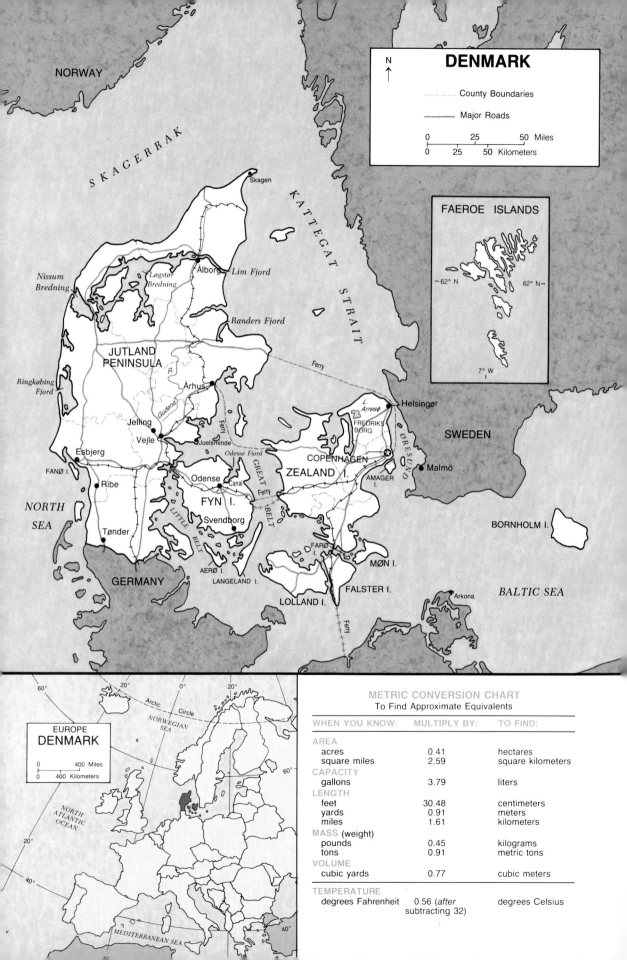

NORWAY

DENMARK

N

County Boundaries

Major Roads

| 0 | 25 | 50 Miles |
| 0 | 25 | 50 Kilometers |

SKAGERRAK

Skagen

KATTEGAT STRAIT

FAEROE ISLANDS

—62° N   62° N—

7° W

Nissum
Bredning

Løgstør
Bredning

Ålborg   Lim Fjord

Randers Fjord

JUTLAND
PENINSULA

Ringkøbing
Fjord

R.
Gudena

Århus

Ferry

L.
Arresø

Helsingør

FREDRIKS-
BORG

ØRESUND

SWEDEN

Jelling

Vejle

Ferry

Juelsminde

Odense Fjord

COPENHAGEN

Malmö

Esbjerg

FANØ I.

GREAT
BELT

ZEALAND I.

Ribe

Odense   Canal

Ferry

AMAGER
I.

NORTH
SEA

FYN I.

LITTLE
BELT

Svendborg

BORNHOLM I.

Tønder

FARØ
I.

AERØ I.

LANGELAND I.

MØN I.

GERMANY

FALSTER I.

Arkona

BALTIC SEA

LOLLAND I.

Ferry

EUROPE
DENMARK

| 0 | 400 Miles |
| 0 | 400 Kilometers |

60°   20°   0°   20°

Arctic Circle

NORWEGIAN
SEA

NORTH
ATLANTIC
OCEAN

60°

20°

40°

MEDITERRANEAN SEA   40°

METRIC CONVERSION CHART
To Find Approximate Equivalents

WHEN YOU KNOW:	MULTIPLY BY:	TO FIND:
AREA		
acres	0.41	hectares
square miles	2.59	square kilometers
CAPACITY		
gallons	3.79	liters
LENGTH		
feet	30.48	centimeters
yards	0.91	meters
miles	1.61	kilometers
MASS (weight)		
pounds	0.45	kilograms
tons	0.91	metric tons
VOLUME		
cubic yards	0.77	cubic meters
TEMPERATURE		
degrees Fahrenheit	0.56 (*after* subtracting 32)	degrees Celsius

Courtesy of John Rice

In their small sailboats, Danes enjoy the waterways that cut through parts of Copenhagen. Old buildings line the harbor of Denmark's main port.

Introduction

The Kingdom of Denmark is a small country in northern Europe. Situated between the North Sea and the Baltic Sea, Denmark has long been an important trading crossroads. Its principal port, Copenhagen, remains a leading international commercial center.

Every place in Denmark—which covers a peninsula and many islands—is close to the sea. As a result, early Danes became sailors and traders. After the Viking era (A.D. 800 to 1050), Denmark became a strong power in the Baltic region, controlling Norway and large areas of Sweden.

From the 1300s through the 1700s, Denmark's expansion was challenged first by German merchants and princes and then by Swedes. By 1814, after many wars with Sweden, Denmark had lost its major territories, including Norway.

Denmark has been a constitutional monarchy since the mid-1800s. Under this system of government, a written constitution guarantees certain rights and provides for an elected legislature. The powers of the Danish monarch are largely symbolic.

Denmark was among the first countries to offer its citizens free public education.

7

Bornholm, the easternmost of Denmark's islands, contains four round churches that served both as religious centers and as military forts in the twelfth and thirteenth centuries.

Independent Picture Service

This and many other social benefits have helped Danes to achieve one of the highest standards of living in the world. The Danish people are heavily taxed to pay for these many programs.

By the late twentieth century, Denmark was prospering economically. Since the mid-1970s, however, it has also struggled to control the price of goods and to decrease unemployment. In addition, the Danes are sharply divided over their country's participation in the European Union (EU), an association of 12 European nations. The future of the Danish economy depends on successful trade with the rest of Europe. Other important goals for the 1990s include maintaining a high quality of life for all Danish citizens and solving economic and environmental problems.

Courtesy of Danish Tourist Board

At a state-run kindergarten, a teacher and her young students work together on an art project. The Danish government funds pre-school education and also supports the country's private schools.

A sturdy windmill graces a farm on the Jutland Peninsula—the largest part of Denmark. Probably used to store or to grind grain, this windmill is old-fashioned compared to the modern, energy-producing types that cluster in windmill parks.

Courtesy of Minneapolis Public Library and Information Center

1) The Land

Denmark is the southernmost of the Scandinavian countries, a grouping that includes Norway, Sweden, and—for some geographers—Finland and Iceland as well. Denmark consists of the Jutland Peninsula, which borders Germany, and more than 400 islands. The country's total land area is 16,630 square miles, which is about twice the size of the state of Massachusetts.

Denmark shares a land border only with Germany, which lies to the south. The North Sea and the Skagerrak—an extension of the North Sea—bound Jutland on the west and north. The Kattegat Strait, which contains Denmark's largest islands, lies to the east. Zealand, the biggest Danish island, sits in the Kattegat, only a few miles off the coast of Sweden. The Baltic Sea lies east of the Danish island of Bornholm.

Denmark has two possessions in the North Atlantic Ocean—Greenland and the Faeroe Islands. Covering an area of

Courtesy of Jill Anderson

Juelsminde, a town on the eastern side of the Jutland Peninsula, is typical of the region's coastal settlements.

Photo © Blaine Harrington III

Bright yellow vegetation—called rapeseed—surrounds a farmhouse on the island of Zealand.

840,000 square miles, Greenland is the largest island in the world. Since 1979, it has been a self-governing province within the kingdom. Most of Greenland lies north of the Arctic Circle and is covered by ice that is up to 11,000 feet thick. The Faeroes—also largely self-governing—are a group of 18 rugged islands located midway between Norway and Iceland.

Topography

With many islands and fjords (sea inlets), Denmark has 4,500 miles of coastline. As a result, no Danish locality is very far from the sea. The country has a low-lying landscape and contains no large wilderness areas.

THE JUTLAND PENINSULA

A region of plains and gently rolling hills, Jutland forms almost two-thirds of Denmark's territory. The peninsula is 200 miles long and about 100 miles across at its widest point. Glaciers once covered northern and eastern Jutland. As these huge masses of slow-moving ice melted, they deposited rich soil on the peninsula and on most of the Danish islands. Soils are poorer in southwestern Jutland, where glaciers did not pass.

The central part of Jutland contains plains and hills. Denmark's highest elevation—Yding Skovhøj (568 feet above sea level)—lies in central Jutland. Running down much of Jutland's western coast to the city of Esbjerg is an almost unbroken row of high sand dunes. From Esbjerg to the German border, a broad, sandy plain spreads to the center of the peninsula.

A number of fjords cut into Jutland's coasts, particularly on the east and west. The Lim Fjord, the deepest and longest fjord, separates northern Jutland from the rest of the peninsula. The fjord extends from the Kattegat Strait westward to Nissum Bredning, a large lagoon with an outlet on the Skagerrak.

THE ISLANDS

Denmark's largest islands are Zealand, Fyn, Lolland, Falster, Bornholm, and Møn. Zealand, the biggest island, is separated from Sweden by a narrow band of water called the Øresund (the Sound). Copen-hagen, Denmark's capital city, faces the Øresund from Zealand's eastern coast.

Fyn, the second largest island, lies between Jutland and Zealand. Two sea channels, the Little Belt on the west and the Great Belt on the east, separate Fyn from Jutland and Zealand. The largest cities on Fyn are Odense and Svendborg.

Lying south of Fyn and Zealand are the islands of Aerø, Langeland, Lolland, Falster, and Møn. White chalk cliffs rising

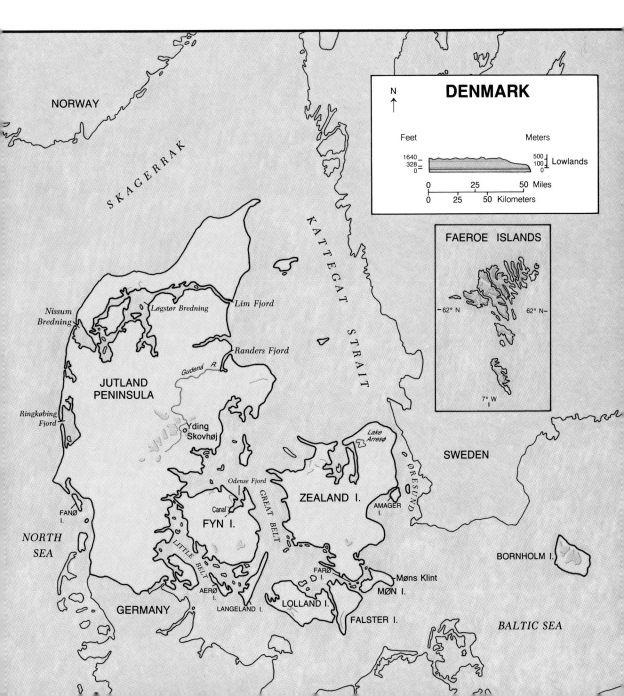

to 400 feet mark the coastline of Møn. Danes call Lolland, Falster, Møn, and the smaller islands nearby the "South Sea Islands."

Situated in the Baltic Sea off southern Sweden is the island of Bornholm. Its granite foundation distinguishes Bornholm geologically from Denmark's other islands, which contain rich, deep soil. Bornholm supplies granite for building purposes. The island also has kaolin, a clay used in making fine china and paper.

Water Resources

Denmark has no large rivers. The longest waterway is the 98-mile Gudenå, which flows through Jutland into the Randers Fjord and the Kattegat Strait. Along with the Gudenå River, several other water-

Møns Klint, a high cliff of chalklike stone, rises on the eastern end of the island of Møn.

Courtesy of Harlan V. Anderson

On a sunny day, people flock to the beaches of Jutland.

Courtesy of Danish Tourist Board

12

Denmark includes many islands, some of which are very far from the mainland. The Faeroe Islands sit northwest of Denmark, midway between Norway and Iceland in the North Atlantic Ocean. Greenland, in the Arctic Ocean, is even farther west. The distance from Copenhagen to the Faeroes is about 930 miles and from the capital to Greenland is roughly 1,500 miles.

ways travel through broad, flat valleys to fjords on the Kattegat. Smaller streams run westward through shallow, steep-sided valleys to the North Sea.

Denmark has many small lakes that formed in basins carved by glacial ice. The largest body of fresh water is Lake Arresø, which covers 16 square miles on Zealand. The country's western coast features several large lagoons with narrow openings to the sea. The largest of these saltwater lagoons are Nissum Bredning and Ringkøbing Fjord. Jutland's Lim Fjord widens as it spreads westward to Nissum Bredning. The fjord's widest section—about 13 miles across—is called Løgstør Bredning.

Climate

Despite Denmark's northerly location, its climate is mild. The seas surrounding the country keep temperatures within a comfortable range. In winter, air masses moving toward Denmark warm up as they pass over the North Atlantic Ocean. In summer, this body of water tends to cool the airstreams. With few hills to push air masses upward, Denmark is usually windy.

Winter temperatures in Denmark generally range between 20° and 40° F. Occasionally the country experiences a very severe winter. About five times each century, prolonged periods of cold in northern Europe have caused the Baltic Sea to freeze over, bringing what the Danes call an "ice winter." Although snowfalls of 24 inches have been recorded, most snows are light and melt fairly quickly. Fog and mist occur frequently. In July, the warmest month, the average temperature is 62° F, but many summer days register thermometer readings above 70° F.

13

Courtesy of Jill Anderson

A swan forages for food in the gardens of Rosenborg Palace in Copenhagen.

Courtesy of Mia Lerner

Short, scrubby vegetation encircles rocks at Helsingør, a castle town on the northeastern tip of Zealand.

14

The country's average annual rainfall is 24 inches. The western coast receives the most moisture, about 31 inches, and the southern islands get the least—16 inches. Storms occur often in summer, and the period from July to December is the rainiest time of the year.

Denmark lies close enough to the Arctic Circle to experience extended periods of daylight—called twilight nights—in June and July. The position of the earth in those months causes the sun to shine continuously in the Arctic. As a result, the skies throughout Scandinavia are bright late into the evening.

Flora and Fauna

Long ago, Danish farmers cleared the country's original forests, mostly stands of oaks and beeches. Trees now cover about 10 percent of Denmark. Many of the woods were planted to block strong winds and to keep soil from eroding. Beech, oak, elm, and linden are the most common trees, but plantations of spruce and fir grow in some areas. Vines—such as yew, holly, and ivy—exist throughout Denmark. Heather (a type of evergreen shrub) thrives wherever forests have been cleared and also dominates the rocky island of Bornholm.

Extensive farming has noticeably reduced the number of mammals in Denmark. Red deer, hares, foxes, and squirrels still make their homes in the woodlands. Denmark's only rabbits live on Fanø, a small island off the western coast of Jutland.

About 300 species of birds inhabit the country during at least part of the year. About 160 of the species, especially waterfowl, breed in Denmark. For centuries, thousands of storks nested in Jutland's marshes and even on the roofs of houses in the town of Ribe. In modern times, storks are rare, partly because many of the marshes in northern Europe have been drained to create farmland.

Photo © Blaine Harrington III

In the North Sea waters off Skagen—the northernmost point on Jutland—a fisherman arranges his catch in the hold of his boat.

Oysters and mussels are found in the Lim Fjord. Saltwater fish in the North Sea include cod, herring, mackerel, and whiting. Those waters also produce large quantities of shrimp. In addition, Danish fishermen catch pouts, sand lances (eels), and sprats—species that are processed for fishmeal, oil, and animal feed.

Copenhagen

About 85 percent of Denmark's people live in urban areas. Because of the country's historic dependence on the sea and shipping, most of the major settlements developed on the coasts. No Danish city, however, rivals the capital of Copenhagen in size and importance.

With 1.4 million people, Copenhagen is Denmark's industrial, educational, and cultural center and also its leading port.

Built in the 1700s, Amalienborg Palace has been a royal residence since 1794. When the monarch is at home, an honor guard is changed at noon to the music of a military band.

Courtesy of Danish Tourist Board

Most of the city sits on the eastern coast of Zealand, but southern Copenhagen extends to the nearby island of Amager. In the 1160s, the Danish king Valdemar I gave the area, which was then a fishing village, to a Roman Catholic archbishop

The Tivoli Gardens opened in 1843 and since then have continued to attract Copenhageners, other Danes, and foreign visitors. At night, lights outline many of the buildings in this popular park.

Independent Picture Service

named Absalon. The settlement that Absalon began there was called *Købmandens Havn,* which means "Merchants' Harbor."

Absalon built a fortress on the island of Slotsholmen. Surrounded by canals in the heart of Copenhagen, Slotsholmen is now the seat of Denmark's government. Christiansborg Palace—where the Danish legislature meets—once housed all of Denmark's governmental offices. In time, ministries in need of more space spread to other buildings on Slotsholmen and into other parts of the city.

Less than a mile north of Christiansborg Palace is Amalienborg Palace, made up of four linked mansions built around a large, eight-sided plaza. The monarch lives in one mansion, and another building is reserved as a home for the heir to the throne. A third residence accommodates visiting royalty, and the fourth mansion provides space for royal administrative offices.

Situated in Copenhagen's commercial district are Tivoli Gardens, a famous park and entertainment complex that opened in 1843. Tivoli offers symphony concerts, ballet, dance halls, a pantomime theater, carnival rides, and restaurants.

As the country's cultural center, Copenhagen is home to the Royal Danish Ballet and many museums. Since the 1970s, the capital has also seen the development of Christiania—a self-sufficient community that took over an abandoned barracks. The small area in east central Copenhagen has attracted many artists and craftspeople.

Photo © Blaine Harrington III

People throng Strøget, the pedestrian street that runs from Copenhagen's Town Hall Square to King's New Market.

Photo © Blaine Harrington III

Inhabitants of Christiania—an independent community in east central Copenhagen—gather outside their homes, which were once a military barracks.

Secondary Cities

Århus, a major port on Jutland's eastern coast, has a population of about 277,000. The city's industries include shipbuilding and the production of machines, beer, and textiles. The ancient city was a bishop's residence in the A.D. 900s, and work on its famous cathedral—which took more than three centuries to build—began in 1201.

Denmark's second largest city, Århus is also a cultural and educational center. The buildings of the University of Århus, whose modern architectural designs have sparked much discussion, sit on parkland that sweeps down to a lake. Botanical gardens in Århus contain Old Town, where small homes from all parts of Denmark were moved and reassembled.

With a population of 183,000, Odense is Denmark's third largest city. The famous storyteller Hans Christian Andersen was born in Odense, which sits on the island of Fyn along the main road from Jutland to Copenhagen. The city's beginnings date from the 900s. Historians think that the site was originally a place where people came to worship the Norse god Odin.

Odense has become an important industrial town, making iron, steel, electronic equipment, textiles, and timber products. The city also has a major shipyard that builds supertankers for international oil companies. A five-mile canal links the city to the Odense Fjord, an extension of the Great Belt.

Ålborg, which sits on the Lim Fjord in northern Jutland, has 159,000 residents. As far back as the eleventh century, the town was an important shipping center. Most of Denmark's trade with Greenland passes through Ålborg's modern port.

Shipbuilding and cement manufacturing are important to the city's economy. Ålborg also produces tobacco and aquavit, a Danish liqueur. St. Botolph's Church, a Gothic structure started in 1430, is one of Ålborg's historic buildings. Another is an ornate, five-storied stone house built in the 1620s by a wealthy merchant named Jens Bang.

Courtesy of John Rice

Reassembled historic dwellings line a street in Århus, Denmark's second largest city. Most of the structures originally came from other areas of the Jutland Peninsula.

With its long seacoasts and many islands, Denmark became a sailing and trading nation early in its history. Among the most successful of the seafaring Danes were Vikings, who used long, fast boats for fighting and commerce.

Independent Picture Service

2) History and Government

Ice from the last Ice Age began to melt and disappear from Denmark by about 12,000 B.C. By 11,000 B.C., nomadic groups had come to the area, probably following reindeer, a source of food and hides. By 3000 B.C., people in Denmark had begun to form permanent settlements. The early settlers farmed the land by burning forests and planting grain in the ashes. These people also raised livestock for food.

About 5,000 years ago, the last of the ice masses melted, causing the sea to flood northwestern Europe. In time, the highest regions became islands that were separated from the other areas of the continent.

Some of these islands eventually became part of Denmark.

Between 2000 and 1500 B.C., newcomers from areas to the east and south took over Jutland. These invaders probably spoke the Germanic language from which modern Danish is derived. They crafted sturdy weapons and fine ornaments from bronze and sailed abroad to trade with other areas of Europe.

By 500 B.C., the inhabitants of Denmark knew how to work iron, which they shaped into strong weapons and tools. Little is known about the next six centuries, but scientists believe a change in climate made

Scandinavia much colder. Trade between Denmark and other parts of Europe declined, as did Denmark's population. Some groups probably emigrated to the south.

After A.D. 100, people in Denmark reestablished trade links with other countries. By the sixth century, the population was growing rapidly, and a number of small kingdoms existed. Some historians believe that around A.D. 500 a people called the Danes came to eastern Denmark from southern Sweden. During the next three centuries, these newcomers built up their kingdom, which in their language was called *Danmark*, meaning "land of the Danes."

The Viking Age

By about A.D. 800, the Frankish Empire to the south was threatening to conquer Denmark. To keep out the Franks, a Danish king built a strong wall across Jutland. The king also led attacks on the Frankish Empire's territory, beginning a period of successful warfare and raids.

Danish sailors and other Scandinavian adventurers—collectively called Vikings—sailed beyond the Baltic and North seas to attack and plunder.

The Viking sea voyages were well organized. Large fleets of light, swift ships carried the raiders on expeditions that surprised and overwhelmed coastal settlements in many parts of Europe. For the next 250 years, separate groups of Danes, Norwegians, and Swedes aggressively sought new territories for conquest and for trading purposes.

Danish and Norwegian Vikings raided lands to the south and west, including the coasts of the British Isles. To save their homes and villages from destruction, the English in some areas paid a bribe—called *Danegeld*—to the invading Danes. In other places in England, Danish Vikings settled and intermarried with the local population. By 886 the English king had recognized an area of Danish settlement—called the *Danelaw*—as an independent region in England under the control of the Danes.

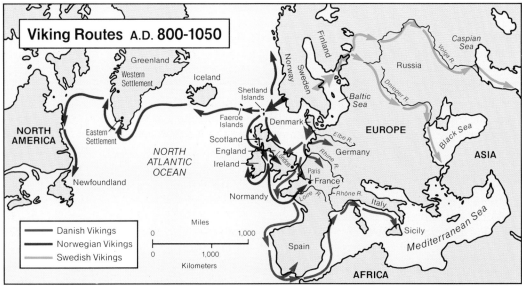

Artwork by Laura Westlund

Between about A.D. 800 and 1050, the Vikings sailed in three main directions from Scandinavia (Denmark, Norway, and Sweden). The Danish Vikings went south, raiding Germany, France, England, Spain, and the Mediterranean coast. The Danes were so successful that by the late ninth century they controlled a large portion of eastern England.

A stone in the town of Jelling commemorates King Gorm the Old and his wife Thyra. He united many of Denmark's small kingdoms in the tenth century. Set up by Gorm's son Harald, the stone carries ancient Scandinavian lettering that also describes Harald's achievements.

Courtesy of Ray Christensen

The Viking age laid the foundation of a Danish nation. By 900 many of the small kingdoms that existed in Denmark had come under the rule of one king, Gorm the Old. After Gorm died, an assembly of free persons, called a *ting,* elected Harald Blå-tand (Bluetooth), Gorm's son, to rule Denmark.

Harald expanded the kingdom and described his success on a stone engraved as a memorial to his father and mother. The symbols on the monument declare that Harald conquered all of Denmark and parts of Norway and made the Danes Christians.

Despite Harald's claim, few Danes were Christians at this time. Most worshiped Norse gods, chiefly Odin, Freya, and Thor. Historians believe that Harald became a Christian to prevent a German ruler from invading Denmark to convert the non-Christian Danes.

A NORTH SEA KINGDOM

Harald's son and successor, Svein I, tolerated the Christian faith but was not himself a Christian. Although Svein did not want German church officials to gain influence in his kingdom, he did not object to Christian missionaries from England working in Denmark. Svein believed that the English represented no threat to his power. Svein's son and heir Canute accepted Christianity and expanded Denmark's territory to include England and Norway. He became king of England in 1016 and completed the takeover of Norway in 1030.

A talented ruler, Canute was accepted by the English and the Norwegians. As a Christian, he strengthened the Roman Catholic Church in Denmark. While Canute was alive, his North Sea kingdom prospered. Shortly after his death in 1035, however, the realm fell apart. Canute's son Hardecanute lost Norway. After Hardecanute died in 1042, the English picked an Englishman as their king.

Denmark acquired a large area of southern Sweden in 1070, when the kings of the two countries established fixed boundaries. This acquisition slowed Danish

Photo by Bettmann Archive

Born in Denmark, King Canute combined Denmark, England, and Norway into a North Sea kingdom in the eleventh century. He returned to his homeland only once after gaining the English throne and died in the English city of Shaftesbury in 1035.

expansion for almost a century. During this time, internal armed conflicts and struggles for the throne disrupted the country. Denmark's political troubles ended when Valdemar I became king in 1157.

Valdemar and Absalon

Valdemar I's chief adviser was Absalon, a childhood friend who became a skilled military and political planner. He was also named a Roman Catholic archbishop. Under the leadership of Valdemar and Absalon, Denmark extended its rule along the southern coast of the Baltic Sea.

At home, Valdemar and Absalon worked to restore the country, which had been weakened by civil wars and high taxation. To build a loyal army, Valdemar granted noble status to any Danish man who could equip himself for military service. In return for serving the king, nobles did not have to pay estate taxes.

During the 25 years of Valdemar's reign, about half the cities of present-day Denmark developed. In 1169 Absalon founded Copenhagen as a fortress on the Øresund —the sea link between the North and Baltic seas. He also strengthened the defenses of the eastern coast and built up Denmark's navy. Absalon founded schools, churches, and monasteries.

Denmark acquired additional territory during the reign of Valdemar's son Canute IV. The aging Absalon, who had become the most powerful person in Denmark, actually ruled for the king. The royal adviser,

Photo by Museum of National History, Frederiksborg

A painting shows Valdemar I standing in full battle dress next to his adviser Bishop Absalon in the German city of Arkona. The bishop is raising his cross as soldiers pull down the statue of a non-Christian god. The Danish king and his friend destroyed Arkona in 1169 to protect Denmark from the Wends, a group of Germanic raiders.

for example, refused to let Canute declare his loyalty to the German emperor, who had demanded this oath under threat of war. Absalon realized that the Germans were busy with other conquests and probably would not fulfill their threat. The Germans did not, in fact, attack.

Conflicts with the Germans

Struggles with German states occurred after Canute's brother, Valdemar II, became king in 1202. He conquered some German lands along the Baltic Sea and overcame Estonia, a Baltic state. Princes in northern Germany struck back within a few years by capturing Valdemar and holding him prisoner for more than three years. To gain his own release, Valdemar had to give up most of the territory he had won.

After Valdemar's death in 1241, Denmark experienced many civil wars as royalty, nobles, and church officials competed for power. In 1282 nobles forced King Erik V to accept a document that limited the monarch's powers.

His son and successor, Erik Menved, tried to reduce the growing power of German merchants, who had formed a trad-

Independent Picture Service

Located on the southern coast of Zealand, Vordingborg Castle includes the Goose Tower, whose spire is topped with the figure of a goose. Valdemar I built the fortress in the twelfth century.

ing organization known as the Hanseatic League. The league—which was made up of commercial cities in Germany and along the Baltic Sea—used its economic strength to gain political power in the region.

Independent Picture Service

The beginnings of Copenhagen date from the reign of Valdemar I, but succeeding Danish monarchs greatly expanded and strengthened the port.

23

While trying to limit the league's influence, Erik Menved amassed a huge debt, which he paid by mortgaging part of Denmark to rich German nobles. For eight years, a German nobleman was the actual ruler of a large portion of Denmark.

In 1340 Erik's grandson Valdemar IV Atterdag became king and began to recapture Denmark's lost lands. In 1361 he conquered the Swedish island of Gotland and its port of Visby, an important Hanseatic city. To strengthen his kingdom, Valdemar IV married a German princess and later engaged his seven-year-old daughter Margrete to the Norwegian king, Haakon VI.

The Union of Kalmar

Struggles between Germans and Scandinavians over land and trade continued throughout the 1300s, even during the calmer reign of Queen Margrete. An intelligent and diplomatic administrator,

Born in 1353, Margrete claimed the throne of Denmark on behalf of her five-year-old son in 1375. While still a young woman, she came to rule Norway and eventually gained power over Sweden. At the time of her death in 1412, her combined kingdom was the largest realm of Europe.

Margrete came to reign over Denmark, Norway, and Sweden.

Her rule of Denmark began in 1375, when she became regent (a person who rules on behalf of another) for her young son Olav II, the grandson of Valdemar IV. After the death of his father, Norway's king Haakon VI, in 1380, Olav became the monarch of Norway. In 1387, after Olav died, Margrete became queen of both Denmark and Norway. In 1389 Swedish officials who wanted to oust their unpopular monarch chose Margrete to govern Sweden as well.

In 1397 Margrete called a conference at Kalmar, Sweden, to formally unite Denmark, Norway, and Sweden. She believed the union would strengthen the countries against the Hanseatic League. At her request, the three governments elected Margrete's grandnephew, Erik of Pomerania, as their king. Margrete continued to rule, however, until her death in 1412.

Erik and the monarchs who followed him were unable to manage the united lands. Denmark, the wealthiest of the three countries, dominated the alliance. The monarch, ruling from Copenhagen, worked to advance Denmark's interests. Although Norway remained part of the Union of Kalmar for four centuries, Sweden attempted many times to break away and rule itself.

In 1448 the Danish council, which consisted of church officials and nobles, elected Christian I as king. He established the House of Oldenburg, the dynasty (family of rulers) that has occupied Denmark's throne ever since. Through his mother, Christian had strong family ties to the German states of Holstein and Schleswig. In time, these territories elected Christian as their leader, beginning a long association with Denmark.

The Protestant Reformation

In the fifteenth century, the Roman Catholic Church in Denmark was powerful and

Christian II, who was elected king in 1513, tried to reduce the power of church officials and nobles. He enacted land reforms and appointed common people as his advisers. The king also sought to reestablish Denmark's authority abroad by invading Sweden. After defeating the Swedish forces, Christian ordered his soldiers to execute 82 Swedish nobles in 1520. Sweden's outrage at the massacre, coupled with a growing desire for independence, led to a final rebellion against Denmark. Within a few years, Denmark's hold on Sweden had been broken.

During the reign of King Frederick I, Christian's uncle, Lutheranism—one of the strongest sects to emerge from the Protestant Reformation—increased its popularity. In Denmark, the sect's main support came from the middle class and from the

Courtesy of Tom Bratvold

According to legend, Denmark's flag—called the Dannebrog—dropped from the sky as a sign of God's favor. The emblem was used in 1397 on the royal seal for the Union of Kalmar, which brought together Denmark, Sweden, and Norway. Considered by some experts to be the oldest flag in Europe, the Dannebrog may resemble the banners of Christian crusaders (religious warriors).

wealthy. The church's large income came from the estates and farms it owned and from the percentage it received of all the grain produced in the country. People began to reject the church as they watched religious officials—most of whom were members of the Danish nobility—amass greater wealth.

In 1479 King Christian I obtained money from the church to build a university in Copenhagen. From the university, the ideas of the Protestant Reformation—a religious movement that challenged the authority of the church—spread throughout Denmark. Opposition to the power of the church and to the nobles grew. In response, Christian's successor, King Hans, called together the first Danish assembly, where the common people were represented along with nobles and church officials.

Photo by Museum of National History, Frederiksborg

Christian II became king in 1513 and put into practice his long-standing opposition to Denmark's wealthy nobles. Conflicts with them and with Sweden occurred frequently throughout his reign, which ended in 1523.

low-ranking clergy. Frederick's death in 1533 brought the religious issue in Denmark to a head. One of his sons, Hans, was a Roman Catholic while the other, Christian, was a Lutheran. The question of which son should rule divided the Danes, and civil war broke out.

Christian III won control of the country in 1536 and established the Lutheran Church as the state church with the monarch as its head. He seized the lands of the Catholic Church, greatly increasing the power and wealth of the crown.

The monarch's wealth soon decreased, however, as Denmark sought to expand its power in the Baltic by fighting battles with Sweden, Russia, and Poland. From 1563 to 1570, Denmark fought the Seven Years' War with Sweden but gained no territory. Denmark then withdrew from military campaigns for the rest of the century. During the decades of peace, prices for the kingdom's exported grain and livestock rose, helping the common people.

Wars Against Sweden

In 1588 King Christian IV began his rule. Young and popular, Christian expanded Copenhagen and constructed many fine buildings, including the Stock Exchange and Frederiksborg Castle. Christian's territorial ambitions for Denmark, however, finally overtaxed the realm's financial resources.

In 1611 Christian IV led Denmark into an unsuccessful and costly war against Sweden. During five years of peace, from 1613 to 1618, Denmark's economy recovered. When the Thirty Years' War (1618–1648) broke out in Germany, Christian IV and his army supported the German Protestants in their conflict against Catholic forces.

Courtesy of Harlan V. Anderson

A painting depicts Christian IV on the deck of his ship, which has just defeated the Swedish navy in a battle on the Baltic Sea. During the attack, an exploding grenade drove a splinter into the king's eye, which he eventually lost. Fought in 1645, this battle was part of the Thirty Years' War—a long conflict that left Denmark defeated and bankrupt.

Christian IV is well known among Danes, perhaps because of the many buildings he constructed in Denmark. One of his creations was Frederiksborg Castle, which was originally a modest country home. The king completely rebuilt the residence in the 1600s. By the time of Christian's death in 1648, the castle had been stripped of its wealth to cover wartime expenses. The building now houses one of Denmark's national museums.

Courtesy of Harlan V. Anderson

In 1626 a defeat in the Harz region of Germany seriously weakened the Danes. Three years later, Catholic forces from Germany occupied Jutland, and Christian IV had to make peace. When Sweden attacked Denmark in 1643, Swedish forces had great success against Danish troops. As a result of these defeats, Denmark became one of the losers in the long conflict.

The treaty that ended the Thirty Years' War in 1648 gave Sweden the island of Gotland and large sections of what is now central Sweden. The war left Denmark's fleet in ruins, its trade seriously damaged, and its treasury empty.

In an effort to keep Denmark out of future wars, the Danish council limited royal powers before electing Christian's son Frederick as monarch. Nevertheless, Frederick III could not resist attacking Sweden in 1657 to regain lost territory. Despite being at war against Poland, the Swedish army marched across the ice-covered Danish islands in the winter of 1658 and forced Frederick to surrender. Denmark lost parts of Norway and all Danish lands east of the Øresund, including the large island of Bornholm.

War soon broke out again with Sweden, and in this conflict the Danes, with help from the Dutch, were more successful. The peace settlement returned Bornholm and central Norway to Denmark, but the other lands east of the Øresund remained Swedish territory.

Return to a Strong Monarchy

The common people blamed the nobles for Denmark's costly wars with Sweden and demanded the right to hold public office. In order to break the nobles' power, Danish commoners were ready to accept increases in royal authority. In 1665 a Danish assembly removed all limits on the king's powers. It adopted a new constitution that made the monarchy hereditary rather than elective. All citizens except peasants were regarded as equal under the rule of the king.

Although Denmark fought against Sweden early in the 1700s, during the remainder of the century the Danes enjoyed a rest from warfare. King Frederick IV, a devout ruler who reigned from 1699 to 1730, encouraged strict obedience to religious practices. The government built schools throughout the country, giving ordinary people access to education. In other respects, however, the lives of peasants worsened.

A law passed in 1733 required all male peasants to spend most of their time on the estates where they were born. Under this system, called *stavnsbånd,* a landowner could sell peasants' services to another landowner. Although peasants had small plots for their own use, responsibilities to the landlords gave the peasants little time to grow crops for their families.

Despite these restrictions on personal liberty, economic conditions for Denmark as a whole had improved by the mid-1700s. Much of Europe was involved in wars, and Denmark's neutrality allowed its trade to flourish. Denmark took over the Caribbean islands of St. Thomas, St. John, and St. Croix, where Danish companies had founded plantations. These estates sold coffee, sugar, and tobacco to European markets. Denmark also traded with Asia, and Copenhagen's importance as a commercial center increased.

Danish society lost some of its religious strictness when Frederick V became king in 1746. More interested in personal pleasures than in ruling, Frederick allowed his ministers to run the Danish government. The strongest leaders were Adam Moltke and J. H. E. Bernstorff. They attempted to reform the farming sector and

The guards that watch over Amalienborg Palace in Copenhagen wear uniforms whose style dates from the nineteenth century.

Courtesy of Jill Anderson

For three days in 1807, the British navy bombarded the capital, leaving few buildings intact. This scene shows the remains of a square in central Copenhagen, with the ruined Churches of Our Lady and of St. Peter in the background.

Photo by Museum of National History, Frederiksborg

to free the peasants. Moltke and Bernstorff also managed to prevent war with Russia by peacefully settling a dispute over Russian claims to Schleswig and Holstein.

Photo by Museum of National History, Frederiksborg

Andreas Peter Bernstorff was Denmark's foreign minister off and on between 1773 and 1797. With the support of Crown Prince Frederick (later Frederick VI), who took over the government in 1784, Bernstorff abolished the restrictive peasant system.

In 1784 Bernstorff's nephew, Andreas Peter Bernstorff, led a new government. In 1788 the younger Bernstorff abolished the stavnsbånd, freeing all peasants. The abolition of the peasant system brought far-reaching changes to Danish agriculture. The government set up a bank to help the former peasants to buy their own farms. Laws forced landlords who rented their holdings to tenant farmers to treat them fairly.

Napoleonic Wars and Democracy

In the 1790s, the French general Napoleon Bonaparte ushered in another era of warfare by trying to conquer Europe. The battles soon interfered with Denmark's trade and neutrality. The British, who were enemies of the French, feared that Denmark's fleet might fall into Napoleon's hands. In 1807, after Denmark refused to turn over its ships to Great Britain, the British navy bombarded Copenhagen and seized the Danish fleet.

The Danish king Frederick VI then formed an alliance with France that lasted until 1814. In that year, forces from Sweden—which was fighting against France—arrived in Jutland and quickly defeated

Independent Picture Service

The ice-bound island of Greenland came under Denmark's authority in the early 1800s at the end of the Napoleonic wars.

the Danish army. Napoleon's loss in 1815 at Waterloo in Belgium ended the Napoleonic wars.

In the negotiations that followed the conflict, Denmark gave Norway to Sweden but kept Norway's former island colonies—Iceland, Greenland, and the Faeroes. The war shattered Denmark's economy and crushed any hopes the country had of becoming a major power in Europe.

Although many Danes believed their king had shown bad judgment by allying with France, they did not immediately try to reduce royal power. The German people who lived in the Danish territory of Holstein, however, demanded their own constitution. In the 1830s, King Frederick responded by allowing landowners to form assemblies in Holstein, Schleswig, Jutland, and the Danish islands. The four assemblies had no lawmaking power, but they gave property owners a place to express their views.

By the 1840s, Danes were demanding educational reforms and representative government. Free, compulsory education was established in 1841. Frederick VII, who became king in 1848, surrendered much of his power on June 5, 1849. On that day, he signed a new constitution that established a two-house Rigsdag (legislature) based on popular representation. The constitution guaranteed freedom of assembly, religion, and the press.

Economic and Political Changes

The German population in Schleswig and Holstein refused to accept the new constitution. The Germans in those areas revolted because they wanted to join other German states in a confederation. Prussia (now partly in modern Germany) and Austria supported Schleswig and Holstein and quickly defeated Denmark in the Danish-German War of 1864. The Treaty of Vienna gave Schleswig and Holstein to Austria and Prussia. The loss of these regions cost Denmark some of its best farmland.

Enrico Dalgas, a young Danish road engineer, thought of a way to make up for the loss of farmland in Schleswig and Holstein. In 1866 he founded an organization to reclaim land from the sea. Farmers drained marshes and planted belts of evergreen trees to prevent soil erosion. Eventually, the farmers cultivated crops in the sandy soil. The land reclamation was so extensive and successful that it made up for the large area that had been lost to the Germans.

During the same period, farmers' groups called cooperatives increased agricultural productivity. Stilling Andersen, a farmer from Hjedding, started the first cooperative. He urged local farmers to process their milk together at a central churning

Reclaiming land from the sea was a major engineering achievement in the 1860s, when Denmark lost the fertile territories of Schleswig and Holstein to foreign powers.

Courtesy of John Rice

station rather than individually on their farms. Andersen demonstrated how members in a cooperative creamery could obtain machinery, research services, and marketing aid that no single farmer could afford. The first cooperative became known for its high-quality products, which sold very well. Other advances in farming soon followed, and the cooperative movement quickly spread throughout Denmark.

A different type of challenge arose in the 1870s, when grain became cheap in Europe. U.S. and Russian farmers, who could produce large quantities of grain very cheaply, dumped their surplus on the European market. European producers could not compete with the cheaper imports, and grain prices fell.

At first, the drop in grain prices hurt Denmark's farmers, but they began to raise more livestock by using the low-cost grain for feed. By the end of the 1880s, Danish cooperatives were shipping large amounts of dairy products and bacon to Britain. By the end of the century, Denmark was a leading exporter of those goods.

Denmark also settled a political disagreement at the end of the 1800s. The country's two major parties—the Conservatives and the Liberals—argued over how much power the Landsting (the upper house of the Rigsdag) and the Folketing (the lower house) should have. The Liberal party dominated the Folketing, and Conservatives controlled the Landsting. The conflict was resolved when a Conservative politician, Jacob Estrup, took over the entire government as prime minister.

The Early 1900s

Backed by King Christian IX, Estrup ran the country until 1894, when loss of political support forced him to resign. The country then began to adopt broad social legislation. The new laws laid the foundation for a welfare state in which the government provided for the basic needs of all

of the nation's citizens. A revised constitution in 1915 granted voting rights to women, lowered the voting age, and abolished special voting privileges for wealthy people.

The Danish economy prospered after 1900. Pigs and dairy cattle became increasingly important to agriculture. The country stepped up its production of iron and steel. Small manufacturers developed high-quality export items, such as silverware and porcelain.

To stimulate trade, Denmark made Copenhagen a free harbor, meaning shippers were not required to pay import taxes when they brought goods into the port. The Danish merchant marine—a fleet of trading ships—grew into one of the largest in the world. Workers formed trade unions

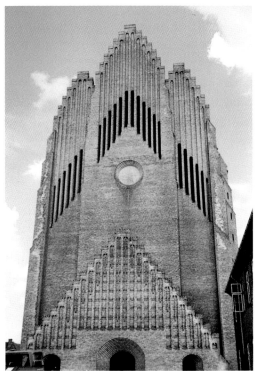

Courtesy of Jill Anderson

Built in the twentieth century, this modern church is named after the nineteenth-century priest, poet, and historian N. F. S. Grundtvig. Founder of the folk-high-school movement, Grundtvig also composed hymns and translated ancient sagas during a period of renewed interest in Danish culture.

Photo by Museum of National History, Frederiksborg

Once a cigar maker, Thorvald Stauning later became a trade unionist and leader of the Social Democratic party. It had a majority of seats in the Danish legislature – the Rigsdag – in the 1920s and 1930s.

to protect their rights, and by 1900 the trade-union movement was well established. Laws protected the workers' right to strike (to stop work as a protest against conditions). As a result of union efforts, Danish industrial laborers doubled their wages between 1875 and 1915.

When World War I broke out in 1914, Denmark declared its neutrality. The war pitted Germany and its supporters against Britain and its allies. In 1918 Germany was defeated. The postwar treaty returned the northern part of Schleswig, which was the home of many Danes, to Denmark.

The 1920s were a time of economic problems for Denmark. Support grew for the Social Democratic party, which wanted the government to help industry and agriculture and also to create jobs by starting large-scale building projects. In 1924 Thorvald Stauning formed Denmark's first government under the Social Democratic party.

Lacking a majority in the Rigsdag, the Social Democrats failed to get their program adopted, and Stauning was soon out of office. With the additional backing of the Radical party, Stauning and the Social Democrats again won a national election in 1929. They stayed in power throughout the 1930s, during a worldwide economic depression. Stauning introduced more social legislation to help the people, but the nation's financial situation continued to decline.

World War II and Its Aftermath

As Denmark was trying to recover economically, other European nations again geared up for war. The German leader Adolf Hitler had rebuilt Germany's military power, which alarmed the Danes. To avoid a conflict, the Danish government signed a pact with Germany in 1939. The pact stated that neither country would attack the other.

Fighting in Europe broke out in 1939, and Germany was again at war with Britain. Denmark declared its neutrality, but Germany did not respect its pact with Denmark. In April 1940, German forces occupied Jutland. Germany justified the action by claiming to protect Denmark from British attacks. German officials said they would not interfere in Denmark's internal affairs if the Danes cooperated.

As the war continued, the Danes increasingly opposed the German occupation. Some Danes demonstrated openly, and others conducted acts of sabotage (destruction) against companies working for the Germans. In August 1943, the Danish government refused to cooperate any longer, and German officials took over the country. German forces occupied Denmark until May 1945, when Germany lost the war in Europe.

Photo by Trustees of the Imperial War Museum, London

Armed Danish resistance fighters watch as defeated German troops pass through Copenhagen's Town Hall Square in May 1945. Germany had occupied Denmark throughout most of World War II (1939–1945).

Photo by Trustees of the Imperial War Museum, London

Danes cheer the British military commander Bernard Montgomery *(waving from a car)* as his victory parade winds through the Danish capital. German troops in Denmark surrendered to Montgomery on May 5. The evening before–while a nationwide blackout was still in force–Danish people throughout the country put small candles in their windows to symbolize their anticipated freedom from German control.

Although Denmark had not been destroyed by the war, the nation's economy had been weakened. The United States provided money to restore Danish industries. The funds allowed Denmark to modernize its factories, to increase industrial output, and to resume trade.

The nation passed a new constitution in 1953 that created a unicameral (one-house) legislature—the Folketing—and made it possible for female members of the royal family to inherit the throne. Denmark became a member of the United Nations and the North Atlantic Treaty Organization (NATO). Participation in NATO —a defensive military organization— marked a shift in Denmark's traditional policy of neutrality.

In 1952 Denmark also helped to establish the Nordic Council, an economic, social, and cultural organization to which Sweden, Norway, Finland, and Iceland also belong. In 1960 Denmark joined the European Free Trade Association (EFTA), an economic group formed by nations that are not in the European Union (EU).

By 1970 Denmark had achieved one of the highest standards of living in the world. Governmental welfare programs made sure all Danes—including the elderly, the sick, and the unemployed—had enough money to live. New policies offered Danish students free schooling at all levels of the educational system. Other laws guaranteed free medical care to all Danes.

Recent Events

Partly because of its welfare costs, Denmark was soon spending more than it was earning. In the early 1970s, the country borrowed more money from foreign countries. To gain economic advantages, Denmark also left the EFTA and joined the EU. A worldwide oil crisis in 1973 and 1974 dramatically increased the cost of imported oil, and Denmark's foreign debt soared. To help pay the debt, the govern-

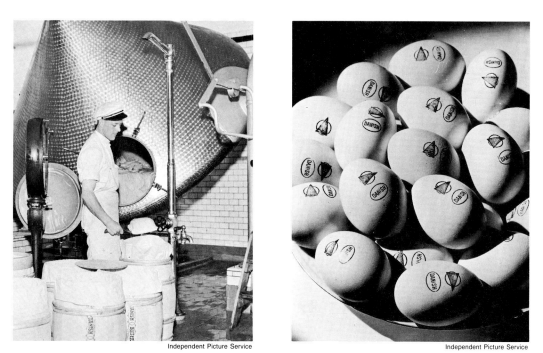

Independent Picture Service

Independent Picture Service

During the 1950s and 1960s, Denmark recovered from its wartime ordeal and rebuilt its farming industries. With new equipment, agricultural cooperatives were producing high-quality butter (left) and eggs (right).

Distribution of Votes
1994 National Election

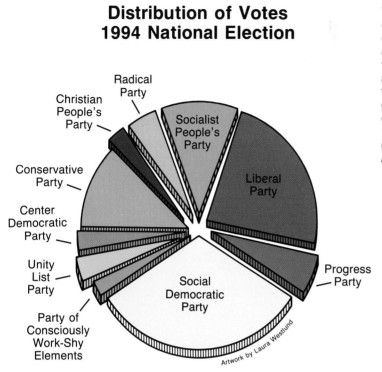

Artwork by Laura Westlund

This pie chart shows the distribution of votes in Denmark's 1994 national elections. No single group received a majority. As a result, three parties—the Social Democratic, the Liberal, and the Center Democratic—combined their strength into a coalition. Together, these parties polled 60.7 percent of the vote and hold 109 of the 179 seats in Denmark's legislature. (Information taken from *The Economist,* 24 September 1994, page 52.)

ment sharply raised taxes, a move that sparked public protests.

In 1982, after many years in power, the Social Democrats lost a national election. No political party dominated the government. Poul Schlüter of the Conservative People's party became prime minister as the head of a coalition (combination) of four parties.

In the late 1980s, Schlüter proposed severe restrictions on public borrowing and spending so that the country could begin to pay off its foreign debt. The state cut back on welfare programs and gave wage increases only to workers who increased their productivity. Laborers helped the government to improve the economy by temporarily accepting smaller wage increases and higher taxes.

In the early 1990s, the EU prepared to eliminate all trade barriers among its member countries. A treaty signed at Maastricht, the Netherlands, set out a plan for creating a single European

currency. Danish voters, fearful that the treaty would rob their country of political and economic independence, initially rejected the treaty.

In 1993 Prime Minister Schlüter resigned from office after a judicial inquiry showed that he had participated in an illegal immigration scheme. Poul Nyrup Rasmussen, leader of the Social Democratic party, formed a coalition with three other parties and became the new prime minister. Rasmussen focused on getting voters to accept the Maastricht treaty. After EU heads excused Denmark from certain parts of the treaty, including the single-currency clause, voters allowed Denmark to sign the agreement in 1993.

Denmark's 1994 election did not yield a majority of votes for any single party. Rasmussen retained support from the three coalition parties that had won seats, and he kept the office of prime minister.

Late in 1996, the supreme court ruled that Denmark's signing of the Maastricht

Photo by © Blaine Harrington III

A craftsman puts the finishing touches on a Scandinavian-style chair *(above)*. **High wages pushed up the prices of Danish products, such as furniture and beef** *(below)*. **As a result, these goods became less competitive on the world market in the early and mid-1980s.**

Photo © Blaine Harrington III

treaty may have been unconstitutional. A lower court must decide if the government has the authority to give up power to the EU. The case is expected to stay in the Danish courts for four to five years, during which time Denmark may not approve any changes to EU economic policy. The delay will affect other EU countries because no action may be taken unless all members agree. The supreme court decision throws into doubt the future of the EU, as well as Denmark's place in the European economic system.

Government

The Kingdom of Denmark is a constitutional monarchy with a parliamentary form of government. This arrangement means the country has a written constitution, a largely symbolic monarch, and an elected assembly that governs the nation. The monarch's main responsibility is to assure that laws passed by the legislature are put into effect. A council helps the ruler in this work.

The lawmaking body is the Rigsdag, which consists of a single house—the Folketing. The Folketing has 179 members, two of whom are from Greenland and two of whom are from the Faeroe Islands.

Most Rigsdag members are elected to represent specific districts, but laws divide 40 of the seats among parties according to the overall number of votes each party gets. For example, a party that wins at

Courtesy of Royal Danish Ministry of Foreign Affairs

To improve overland transportation, the Danish government funded the building of the Farø Bridge in the 1980s. It links the small island of Farø with Zealand and Falster.

Queen of Denmark since 1972, Margrethe II *(pictured with her husband and two sons)* has a largely symbolic role in the government of the kingdom.

Courtesy of Royal Danish Ministry of Foreign Affairs

least 2 percent of the national vote may send at least one delegate to the Folketing. This system has encouraged many parties to organize. All Danes over the age of 18 can vote, and voter turnout is high.

The prime minister, who is a member of the Rigsdag, is usually the leader of the dominant party in the governing coalition. The prime minister heads a cabinet in which each minister is responsible for specific areas of government. The cabinet ministers are chosen from the main parties in the Rigsdag.

Cabinets may stay in power for up to four years before a national election must be called. The Folketing sometimes passes a vote of "no confidence" when a majority of its members do not agree with the cabinet's decisions. In that case, the prime minister resigns or asks the monarch to call for a new election.

Denmark's highest court is the supreme court, on which 15 judges serve. Serious criminal cases are first heard before one or two high courts. The cases are tried before a jury of 12 people and a panel of at least 3 judges. If the jury reaches a verdict of guilty, the judges can overrule the jury. If the jury decides a defendant is innocent, however, that decision is final. The judges and jury cooperate in setting sentences for convicted criminals.

Denmark contains 16 governmental units—14 counties and the municipalities of Copenhagen and Frederiksborg. The 14 counties are further divided into 275 municipalities. Voters at each level of local government elect a council, and the council chooses a mayor to run the municipality or county.

Independent Picture Service

A statue of King Frederick VII, who established the Rigsdag in 1849, stands in front of Christiansborg Palace, where the legislature meets.

Photo © Blaine Harrington III

A group of happy Zealander college students waves Danish flags on graduation day. The graduates proudly wear the white caps that symbolize they have passed their final exams.

3) The People

About 85 percent of Denmark's 5.2 million people live in urban areas. Residents of the countryside are evenly distributed among farms, forest plantations, and fishing villages. The density of the population is about 309 people per square mile, which is much greater than in any other Scandinavian country.

Most Danes are descended from Germanic peoples. One Dane out of 13 has Jensen for a last name. Nielsen and Hansen are also common names. Danish is the principal language, but a small German-speaking minority lives in southern Jutland.

Way of Life

For the past two centuries, Denmark has worked to make sure that its citizens have equal opportunities and good incomes. Denmark's average income per person in the early 1990s was about $15,000. Most Danes work 39 hours per week and receive five weeks of paid vacation each year. Their country has virtually no slums and few poor people. In recent years, the workers and the government have cooperated to hold down wage increases in an effort to solve economic problems.

In summer, many urban residents escape to rural cottages for long vacations. Others travel to tourist spots in other parts of Europe. "Colony gardens," first used in the late 1880s, are popular weekend retreats for city dwellers. These rented plots of land allow urban Danes to grow flowers, fruits, and vegetables and even to maintain small greenhouses near the nation's cities.

"Colony gardens"—small plots of rented land—give urban Danes a chance to grow their own fresh food outside the cities.

Photo © Blaine Harrington III

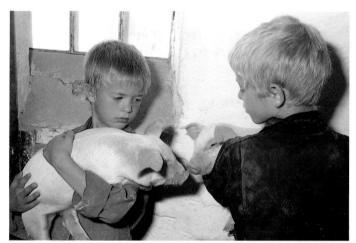

Courtesy of Danish Dairy Board, Inc.

The children of a Danish hog farmer hold two growing piglets. About 80 percent of the meat from pigs raised in the country is exported.

Courtesy of Danish Tourist Board

People young and old enjoy the rides at Legoland, an amusement park on Jutland.

Men and women have equal rights by law, but women often earn less money from their jobs. Not many women serve as governmental officials, but women are members of the courts, the cabinet, and the Rigsdag. Women can also become ministers in Denmark's Evangelical Lutheran Church.

Most couples in Denmark live together before marriage. Many who do marry elect to have a "paperless marriage," meaning they do not participate in formal ceremonies. A law passed in 1988 gives homosexual couples the same legal status as heterosexual married couples.

Education

Denmark was one of the first countries in the world to require children to attend school. Elementary education lasts for nine years, but many students opt for a tenth year. Elementary students do not

Courtesy of Danish Tourist Board

These young Danes spend their mornings at a day-care center funded by the Danish government.

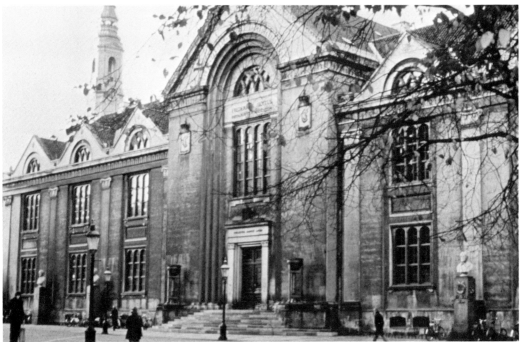

Courtesy of Danish Tourist Board

Denmark has five universities and many other institutions that offer classes to high-school graduates. The oldest university is in Copenhagen and has expanded in recent years as more young Danes enroll in a variety of courses.

To the accompaniment of an accordion, older Danes exercise at a state-run nursing home.

Courtesy of Danish Tourist Board

take examinations at the end of each grade level. They can, however, take a test at the end of their schooling if they want to receive a final grade. About 91 percent of Danish children attend public school. The remainder enroll in private schools, for which the government pays 85 percent of the expense.

During three years at the secondary level, young people study subjects that emphasize either language skills or mathematics. After basic schooling, two-thirds of the students go to specialized schools for technical or commercial education. Students must pass final examinations before they can enter universities.

Denmark has five universities, the oldest of which is the University of Copenhagen, which was established in 1479. The newest university opened in 1974. Additional schools of higher learning provide advanced degrees in engineering, pharmacy, dentistry, architecture, veterinary science, and other specialties.

Another feature of the Danish educational system is the residential folk high schools, which are privately operated. The historian N. F. S. Grundtvig founded the first folk high school in 1844. His aim was

to cultivate in young people, especially those from rural areas, an interest in social and political problems and to give young Danes a chance to develop special talents. After starting in Denmark, the folk-high-school movement spread throughout Scandinavia.

Health and Welfare

In return for the high taxes they pay, Danes receive many social and welfare benefits from the government. The public-health system provides free medical care and hospitalization and pays for medications and some dental services.

Life expectancy at birth for a Dane is very high—75 years. During the 1980s, the birthrate was low, and the government predicted that the population would begin to decline within a few years. Instead, a slight rise in the birthrate in 1990 indicated that the population might remain stable or even grow slightly.

Retired persons receive pensions that rise as the cost of living increases. Governmental programs help the elderly to remain in their own houses for as long as possible. Retirees who require care can

43

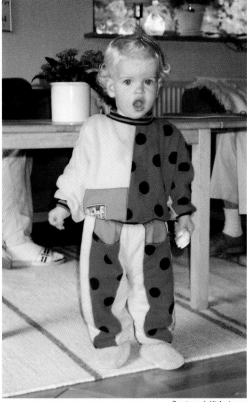

Courtesy of Jill Anderson

Children in Denmark receive excellent care even before they are born. In addition, until the age of 13, free vaccinations against polio, whooping cough, and other childhood diseases are standard practice. Free dental care is available until age 18.

move to public nursing homes, where each resident has a private room.

The government also provides insurance to cover unemployment and the expenses of work-related injuries. Training and re-training programs prepare persons without jobs to find work. The state gives special assistance to the disabled. Public day-care centers meet the needs of working parents.

Religion and Festivals

Although 90 percent of the Danish people officially belong to the state church—the Evangelical Lutheran—regular attendance at Sunday services is low. Danes may stop being members of the church at any time. The monarch is the only Dane required by law to belong to the state church. Members pay an annual tax to support the work of the Lutheran churches throughout Denmark.

Lutheran clergy baptize four out of five Danish children, perform half of the marriage ceremonies, and conduct most funerals. Other religious groups in Denmark include the Swedish Church, the Russian Orthodox Church, the Church of England, the Roman Catholic Church, and the Reformed Church.

Danes celebrate many holidays, most of which are observed with hearty meals of special foods. Rice pudding topped with raspberry sauce is usually served as the first course on Christmas Eve. A single almond is buried in the pudding, and the person who finds the almond receives a gift.

Courtesy of Her Majesty Queen Margrethe II

Queen Margrethe II designed this stamp, which commemorates the fortieth anniversary of Denmark's liberation from German occupation during World War II. Lighted candles are set on windowsills as part of the annual celebrations for Liberation Eve (May 4).

Another Danish Christmas tradition is to hang a stalk of corn on the door or to spread grain for the birds. Children anticipate the arrival of the Christmas troll, who brings gifts.

On Liberation Eve (May 4) homes display lighted candles in windows to commemorate Denmark's liberation from German occupation at the end of World War II. Liberation Day (May 5) is a national holiday, as is Constitution Day on June 5. On Midsummer's Eve, Danes light bonfires to celebrate the arrival of the longest day of the year.

Since 1912, Danes have also celebrated the anniversary of U.S. independence on July 4 in Ålborg's Rebild National Park. In that year, U.S. citizens of Danish descent bought land for the park. They gave the park to the Danish government under the proviso that the Fourth of July be celebrated there each year.

Language and Literature

The Danish language grew from the Germanic tongues once spoken in many parts of northern Europe. By the twelfth century A.D., the languages used in Scandinavia had broken into two historical groups—West Scandinavian and East Scandinavian. In the first division were Norwegian and Faeroese. In the second grouping were Swedish and Danish. Modern Danish, Swedish, and Norwegian, however, are very similar.

Throughout its long history, Danish has been influenced by outside forces. The arrival of Christianity brought in new words and the use of the Latin alphabet. Contact with the Hanseatic League introduced many German words. Danish dialects developed as differences grew between city dwellers and rural people. By about 1700, however, a standard spoken Danish, called *Rigsmålet,* was in use. Reforms in the late 1800s produced a standard written Danish, known as *Rigssproget.*

Denmark has produced a number of great writers and scholars. Ludvig Holberg, considered the founder of Danish literature, wrote comic plays in the 1700s that criticized Danish society. He also authored serious historical works and helped to shape Danish into a national language through his poetry.

Among the most famous Danish writers is Søren Kierkegaard, who lived from 1813 to 1855. He is known as the Father of Existentialism. Existentialists believe that,

Simple, white-washed churches dot the landscape of rural Denmark. This example lies in northeastern Falster, an island south of Zealand.

Courtesy of John Rice

45

through constant questioning and choosing, people can take responsibility for their own existence. Kierkegaard argued that belief in God or religion cannot be supported by reason but rather is an act of faith. Although he was a Christian, Kierkegaard frequently criticized the Evangelical Lutheran Church, saying that its members had not really examined the basis of their beliefs.

The works of Hans Christian Andersen, who was born in 1805, are among the most widely translated and read in the world. The Danish storyteller's most famous fairy tales include *The Little Mermaid, The Ugly Duckling,* and *The Emperor's New Clothes.* Although funny and entertaining, Andersen's writings also give insight into human behavior, based on the author's keen observations of people and society.

Throughout the second half of the 1800s, Danes produced many realistic

Independent Picture Service

In 1868 the storyteller Hans Christian Andersen was photographed reading to a group of young Danes. Famous worldwide as the author of many popular fairy tales, Andersen also wrote adult plays and novels. His stories, including *The Ugly Duckling,* are often heavily illustrated (above left). *The Little Mermaid,* a statue on Copenhagen's harbor, commemorates another one of Andersen's tales.

Independent Picture Service

46

Leading contemporary writers include Marianne Larsen and Vita Andersen, whose books focus on women's changing roles in society. Klaus Rifbjerg has written many modern novels, plays, poems, and filmscripts.

The Arts

Ballet is an art form long associated with Denmark. The Danish dancer and teacher Auguste Bournonville founded the Royal Danish Ballet in 1829 and directed it until 1879. The company continues to perform throughout the world.

Denmark's foremost musical composer was Carl Nielsen, who died in 1931. Among Nielsen's compositions were six symphonies and two operas. In recent years, Danish jazz musicians have earned an international reputation for their compositions and performances. Victor Borge, a Dane who has entertained audiences throughout the world, works his musical talent into comedy routines.

Independent Picture Service

Born in 1885, the novelist Karen Blixen used the pen name Isak Dinesen and wrote books in both English and Danish. After her marriage in 1914, Blixen moved to a coffee plantation in Kenya, Africa. Many of her fictional works have historic European settings, but her first book of memoirs, *Out of Africa,* reflects her experiences in Kenya. She returned to Denmark in 1931 and died there in 1962.

works. The writers included Jens Peter Jacobsen, Hermann Bang, and Henrik Pontoppidan. Karen Blixen, who wrote under the name Isak Dinesen, was born in 1885 to an upper-class Danish family. After marrying a Swedish nobleman, she moved to a farm in Africa. Blixen's experiences there formed the basis of novels and memoirs, including *Out of Africa.*

In addition to Blixen, an important figure in Danish literature after 1900 was Johannes V. Jensen, who received a Nobel Prize in 1945 for his novel *The Long Voyage.* The clergyman and playwright Kaj Munk began writing plays in the 1930s. Deeply influenced by Kierkegaard, Munk believed that humans were doomed because of their basic sinfulness. During World War II, he strongly opposed the Germans, who murdered him in 1944.

Independent Picture Service

The Danish composer Carl Nielsen grew up on the island of Fyn. His works—which include symphonies, concertos, and chamber music—often rely on complex harmonies.

47

Courtesy of Royal Copenhagen Ltd.

Following the historic pattern called *Flora Danica* (Danish Flower), an artisan at the Royal Copenhagen Manufactory hand paints the lid of a serving bowl. One of the world's most famous porcelain patterns, Flora Danica dates from 1790, when the Danish monarch owned the factory.

A silversmith skillfully hammers a tray by hand at the Georg Jensen works in Copenhagen.

Courtesy of Royal Copenhagen Ltd.

Denmark has many theaters for dramatic productions. In Copenhagen are the Royal Theater and the Tivoli Concert Hall. The courtyard of Kronborg Castle in Helsingør is the site for annual performances of the Shakespearean play *Hamlet,* which is about a Danish prince from Helsingør. Shakespeare based his story on a folk legend recorded in *Gesta Danorum* by Saxo Grammaticus, Denmark's first historian, who wrote in the 1100s.

Simplicity and elegance characterize Danish design in silver, porcelain, glass, pewter, and textiles. In the 1930s, Danish artists led the way in creating a uniquely Scandinavian type of furniture that is comfortable and that uses simple shapes. This style has carried over into other items for everyday use.

Denmark's most famous porcelain maker is the Royal Copenhagen Manufactory, which the Danish monarch once owned. Danish silverware is associated with Georg Jensen, who established his company in 1904. His designs were simple and elegant rather than ornate and fancy, and his company still makes high-quality tableware in Copenhagen.

Actors from the Royal Theater of Copenhagen *(below)* perform a scene from an eighteenth-century comedy. Another cultural attraction in the capital is the Royal Danish Ballet *(right)*.

Independent Picture Service

Independent Picture Service

A Danish glassmaker carefully engraves a vase with geometric designs.

Independent Picture Service

Food

The Danish people enjoy good food and warm hospitality. Most Danes eat four meals a day. A cold breakfast is followed by lunch, then a hot dinner, and finally a late supper.

Danish bakers are known for their fine pastries, including buttery almond cakes and *kringles* (coffee cakes). An open-faced sandwich called a *smørrebrød* can be a whole meal. The sandwich consists of a thin slice of buttered bread topped with smoked salmon, tongue, ham, eggs, or cheese and trimmed with herbs and pickles. Danish cooks take great pride in the appearance and presentation of food. As a result, smørrebrøds may be decorated with twists of cucumber, tomato, beets, citrus fruit, or onion rings.

When Danes dine in restaurants, their favorite menu choices include meatballs, roast pork with red cabbage, venison with berries, and grilled sausages. Danes drink little wine, but the average annual consumption of beer is 40 gallons per person—the highest in Scandinavia. Aquavit, a spiced Danish liqueur, is popular as an after-dinner drink.

Denmark is famous for its cheeses, particularly Danish blue cheese. Light yellow Havarti cheese was invented by a Danish farmer in the nineteenth century. Very smooth in texture, Havarti develops large and small holes while the cheese is aging. Samsoe is a bland cheese that many Danes eat every day. Danbro cheese contains caraway seeds, and Esrom has a buttery texture.

Courtesy of Burch Communications, Inc.

In Danish homes, rice pudding smothered by a tasty raspberry sauce is a favorite cold dish at Christmastime.

Photo © Blaine Harrington III

The restaurant in Copenhagen's central train station offers a wide variety of Danish specialties in an attractive and colorful buffet.

Independent Picture Service

Games of football (soccer) draw large crowds in Denmark. Volunteers run football clubs throughout the country, developing the talents of young Danish players.

Courtesy of Hans Hansen Koed

Danes are introduced to water sports at an early age. Most cities are close to the sea, and people have many opportunities to sail, row, and swim.

Sports and Recreation

Denmark's national sport is soccer, which Danes call *fodbald*. Danish amateurs also compete in soccer, and the country contributes many players to European professional teams. About 300,000 Danes of all ages play soccer. In the spring of 1992, Denmark's team scored a surprising victory in the European soccer championship.

In the Olympic Games and at other international competitions, Danes have excelled in water sports. Easy access to the sea and to many lakes encourages Danes to learn sailing, sculling (rowing), and swimming. Other sports favored by Danes are badminton, tennis, handball, archery, and fencing.

Many Danes participate in athletic activities for exercise rather than for competition. Jogging and cycling are very popular, and long-distance races draw thousands of participants. Other Danes compete at a card game called bridge or in chess. Bent Larsen, who became a chess grandmaster at the age of 21, has won many international tournaments.

Members of Denmark's German-speaking minority participate in a horse-riding event in Tønder, a city in southwestern Jutland.

Courtesy of John Rice

53

Long a seafaring nation, Denmark continues to make and repair ships. Here, workers wash the hull of a tanker in Copenhagen's port.

Photo © Blaine Harrington III

4) The Economy

Once reliant on farming for most of its income, Denmark now has many industries. Farm products, however, are still an important part of the nation's exports, accounting for about 25 percent of foreign earnings. Small and medium-sized companies make most of the manufactured goods.

Denmark has no raw materials of commercial value, except for salt and recently discovered oil and gas in the North Sea. For that reason, the country has developed only a few heavy industries. As a small country with a limited domestic market, Denmark has prospered by trading with other nations. Many Danish companies depend on foreign customers for most of their sales and profits. For this reason, the plans for unifying the European market will have a strong impact on the Danish economy.

Laborers are well organized in Denmark. About 85 percent of Danish workers belong to labor unions—one of the highest percentages in the world. Negotiation and compromise over wage changes have prevented many strikes. Nevertheless, high unemployment remains a serious problem in Denmark, where 12.5 percent of the work force was jobless in 1994.

Manufacturing

About 20 percent of the work force is employed in the manufacturing sector. Almost all Danish industries are privately owned. The government operates the postal service, the gas and electric utilities, some transportation companies, and certain other services on which the country depends. Foreign corporations own about one-twelfth of Denmark's businesses.

Danish firms are small, with an average of 60 employees. Almost half of the businesses have fewer than 20 workers. In the late 1980s, large companies bought smaller ones, particularly within industries that produced food and beverages.

Many Danish manufacturers are anticipating possible economic changes in the

Photo © Blaine Harrington III

A factory on the Jutland Peninsula produces canned hams. Food processing is a major manufacturing activity.

1990s. Denmark's refusal to participate fully in the Maastricht treaty—which would create a single currency in Europe—may lead to isolation for Danish exporters, and higher prices for importers.

Forklifts help to load stacks of beer from the Carlsberg Brewery in Copenhagen.

Photo © Blaine Harrington III

Hand-crafted furniture—featuring the sleek, simple style called Scandinavian—attracts buyers from around the world.

Independent Picture Service

The largest Danish manufacturing sectors are steel, chemicals, food processing, and machinery. Danish companies also manufacture consumer goods, including clothing, appliances, and furniture.

One of the world's largest exporters of beer and a leading producer of diesel engines are both Danish firms. Parents from many parts of the world buy their children building blocks made in Denmark. A Danish company is the world's largest supplier of insulin, a drug used by people suffering with diabetes. Tableware, linens, and other household items from Denmark also attract customers worldwide.

Agriculture

About 6 percent of the Danish work force is employed in the agricultural sector, and

Dairy farms are decreasing in number in Denmark, as many farmers switch to raising beef cattle.

Courtesy of Danish Dairy Board, Inc.

A worker in a cheese-making factory turns rows of Danish cheese as they age.

Courtesy of Danish Dairy Board, Inc.

two-thirds of Denmark's land is devoted to farming. Single families own and operate most of the farms. Laws prohibit non-farmers from holding title to agricultural land.

Because of the soil's fertility, a favorable climate, and advanced agricultural methods, Danish farms are extremely productive. On the average, each worker raises enough food to feed 100 people. The coun-try meets all of its own food needs and sells about 70 percent of its farm products abroad.

Danish agriculture changed rapidly after World War II, when two-thirds of the small farms merged to form large farms. These estates, however, are still small compared to those throughout most of Europe. In the four decades since the war, urban and suburban developments, airfields,

Courtesy of John Rice

Typical of a Danish farm building, this barn on the island of Falster houses about 180 cows.

Photo © Blaine Harrington III

Courtesy of Danish Dairy Board, Inc.

Although farmers grow some grains (left), **most of Denmark's farming sector is devoted to raising high-quality pigs** (right).

roads, and industries claimed about 10 percent of the farming area. Most of this land was in the fertile eastern part of Denmark. Despite the loss of rich farmland, yields per acre rose steadily because of new seed strains, better fertilizers, improved drainage, and other advances.

Most cultivated land in Denmark provides grain to nourish animals, but some fields are used to grow barley—the most important cereal crop. Oats and rye are also planted. For years, Danish livestock producers raised mostly pigs and dairy cattle. A shortage of agricultural workers in recent years has encouraged more farmers to switch to raising beef cattle, which require less labor. About 300 agricultural producers in Denmark specialize in poultry, meeting the country's demand for eggs, chickens, and turkeys. Surplus poultry is exported.

Fishing

Denmark ranks among the world's top 10 fishing nations in terms of the value of its catch. Individuals who use their own boats—rather than companies that own fleets—carry out nearly all of the fishing activity. Danish fishermen mostly work in the North Sea. Hauls of cod are sold for food, and sand lances are processed for animal feed. The country's main fishing port is at Esbjerg in western Jutland.

In recent years, overfishing has caused shortages of fish in the North Sea. The sea's herring population, for example, has dropped dramatically, and a ban on large-scale herring fishing is in effect. To protect the fishing industry, Denmark, Norway, Sweden, and other countries have agreed to restrict their fishing activities. With a smaller area to fish, the Danes find it increasingly difficult to earn a living at sea.

Fishing has long been a source of income for Danes. Decreases in the yearly catch, however, have made this job more difficult in recent years.

Courtesy of Jill Anderson

Photo © Blaine Harrington III

Small, family-owned boats accomplish most commercial fishing in Denmark. This vessel is heading for the North Sea from the port of Esbjerg, which lies on the western coast of the Jutland Peninsula.

59

Boxes of fish are lined up at an auction for public sale.

Independent Picture Service

About 600 inland fish farms provide freshwater trout to Danish tables.

Transportation and Shipping

Denmark has a well-developed transportation system that includes roads, railways, ferries, air services, and bridges. About two Danes in five own a car. More than half the population uses bicycles to get around on short trips. A state-owned railway operates both train and bus services throughout the country. Ferries that can hold 2,000 passengers and up to 400 cars travel regularly between Zealand and Fyn and between Jutland and Zealand.

Denmark is building a 10.5-mile bridge and tunnel across the Great Belt to connect Zealand and Fyn. The project will cost at least $3 billion and will accommodate both trains and vehicles when completed in 1997. A 2-mile-long bridge from southern Zealand to Falster lengthens the major highway between Scandinavia and Germany. Ferries complete the system. A bridge between Copenhagen and Malmö, Sweden, is expected to be built by 2000.

With Sweden and Norway, Denmark owns the international Scandinavian Airlines System (SAS), which flies throughout Europe, to the United States, and to other parts of the world. Danair runs flights from Copenhagen to other parts of Denmark. Other Danish airlines provide mostly charter flights. Copenhagen's airport is the fifth largest airfield in Europe and handles flights from almost all international airlines.

About 600 privately owned vessels form Denmark's merchant fleet, whose huge, modern ships and tankers move products around the world. The biggest Danish shipping company owns 100 vessels and is one of the largest shippers in the world.

Energy

In the early 1970s, Denmark depended on imported oil for 93 percent of its energy needs. After the international energy crisis of the mid-1970s, most Danish power

Courtesy of Harlan V. Anderson

Ferries transport people and goods between the more than 400 islands in Denmark. Some of the boats are large liners, while others can accommodate only a few cars.

Courtesy of Danish Tourist Board

The Danish State Railways runs the nation's train services, which cross from island to island with the help of ferries.

Windmill technology is advanced in Denmark, where the low-lying terrain and lack of mountains welcome the winds that produce electricity.

Courtesy of Minneapolis Public Library and Information Center

plants began using coal rather than oil. As the decade continued, the country developed its own oil and natural gas supplies from fields discovered in Denmark's sector of the North Sea. By the early 1990s, the fields were providing two-thirds of Denmark's oil and gas and meeting nearly one-half of its overall energy needs.

Danes have been unwilling to build nuclear power facilities because of the environmental hazards they pose. The energy crisis also encouraged individual Danes to conserve fuel, which has helped to reduce oil consumption.

The Danes' interest in nonpolluting sources of energy has made the country a leader in the development of windmill technology. Thousands of tall, modern windmills that harness power from moving air dot the Danish countryside. Some are concentrated in windmill parks that supply local needs and sell surplus electricity to traditional power networks.

The Future

Although Denmark has adapted its economy to modern needs and boasts a wide range of social benefits, the nation continues to face problems. Chief among these are unemployment and high prices for goods. The Danish people, however, have shown a willingness to accept short-term hardships to help the economy recover.

For example, workers in recent years have agreed to wage increases that are lower than those received by laborers in other industrialized countries. This situation has enabled Danish companies to hold down prices for their products and to remain competitive in world markets.

In the late 1980s, Danes also cooperated in the government's plan to cut spending and to raise taxes, even though these measures hurt consumers and temporarily lowered the standard of living. As a result of these sacrifices, the country exported more goods, and for the first time in many years Denmark's economy seemed to be making measurable progress.

Danish producers still face competition at home from other European manufacturers. The unification of the European market may hurt the ability of small businesses to compete. In addition, many Danes oppose foreign control and influence in the country's political system.

Denmark's struggle over the EU's Maastricht treaty may hurt the country's economy and its relations with other nations. The EU, which plans to establish a unified market with a single currency, will have trouble proceeding without Denmark. The Danes' reluctance to cooperate with the treaty could affect economic conditions not only in Denmark, but throughout Europe. The country must reconcile its concerns about national sovereignty with the responsibilities of EU membership.

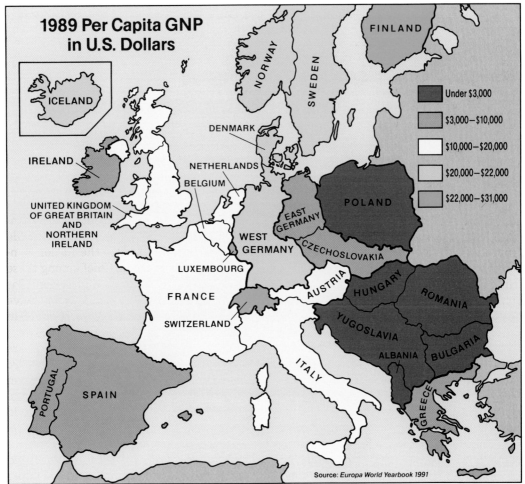

1989 Per Capita GNP in U.S. Dollars

■	Under $3,000
■	$3,000–$10,000
□	$10,000–$20,000
▨	$20,000–$22,000
▨	$22,000–$31,000

Source: *Europa World Yearbook 1991*

Artwork by Laura Westlund

This chart compares the average productivity per person—calculated by gross national product (GNP) per capita—for 26 European countries. The GNP is the value of all goods and services produced by a country in a year. To arrive at the GNP per capita, each nation's total GNP is divided by its population. The resulting dollar amounts indicate one measure of the standard of living in each country. Denmark's 1994 figure of $28,110, combined with strong government-welfare programs, means that Danes continue to live comfortable, healthy lives.

Index